Someone Always in the Corner of My Eye

Someone Always
in the
Corner of My Eye

Bo-Seon Shim

Translated by
Daniel Parker & YoungShil Ji

WHITE PINE PRESS / BUFFALO, NEW YORK

White Pine Press
P.O. Box 236
Buffalo, New York 14201
www.whitepine.org

Publication of this book was made possible, in part, by grants from
the Literature Translation Institute of Korea.

Cover art: "Revert 14" by Hyung Sook Oh. Copyright ©2016 by
Hyung Sook Oh. Used by permission of the artist.

First Edition

Korean Voices Series, Volume 22

ISBN: 978-1-935210-90-0

Printed and bound in the United States of America.

Library of Congress Control Number: 2015959244

Ad Mundi / To the World

Contents

Part II

Poetry, you ask me only once, but
I answer you eternally.

—BoSeon Shim
August 2011

Foreword

"One good thing I've done today was…" In the first line of his poem "Good Things," Bo-Seon Shim presents his mission as a poet and a sociologist. In this collection of poems – which include deeply personal poems, lyric experiments, and strong social statements – the reader is constantly challenged to discover the "one good thing" that is possible from each day.

Someone Always in the Corner of My Eye is a collection that reflects the voices of a community. Friends, lovers, family, and even blind foreigners are portrayed in this collection. He presents grandiose illusions and underprivileged whispers, assures us, and challenges us to consider our relationships, even our connection to a dead locust.

Born in Seoul in 1970, Shim received his Ph.D. in sociology from Columbia University after graduating from Seoul National University in Seoul, South Korea. He made his poetic debut in the Chosun Ilbo Annual Spring Literary Contest in 1994, and his first collection of poems (*Seulpeumi opneun sip o cho*, or *Fifteen Seconds Without Sorrow*) was published in 2008. This collection (Originally *Nunape opneun saram* in Korean) was originally published in 2011. A prose collection (*Geueurin yesul*, or *Smoked Art*) was published in 2013 and has yet to be translated into English. His work has been published in numerous anthologies including anthologies of Literary Award winners. and has also appeared in a collaborative book of poetry and four books of prose.

Shim has received the Nojak Literary Award and the JoonSeong Kim Literary Award. His prose collection was named the Humanities Book of the Year in 2013. Professor of Culture and Management at Kyung Hee Cyber University, Shim is a member of the 21st Century Prospect Writer's Group. He is a contributing editor for *F*, the arts and humanities magazine.

During a 2013 discussion with the translators, Shim said he prefers not to use the words "romantic" or "manifesto" to describe his poems, but there is no denying that many of Shim's poems express deep emotions and/or take a clear stand on social and economic issues. Even when he describes deeply personal relationships — friendships, lovers, or intellectual equals — there is purpose as well as passion.

As a sociologist/poet, Shim understands that the world is filled with unstable relationships. At the same time, he realizes that he is a passenger on a journey to try to figure out the answers. "The humble and lively dreams we pursue in the middle of our lives," he says, "sometimes provide a place to work against the social roles and functions that we are assigned."

Welcome to Shim's humble and lively dreams.

— YoungShil Ji and Daniel T. Parker

Part I

Words

There is countless evidence that we have souls.
Today I will reveal one truth.
And tomorrow, another.
Like that, one each day.

Scratching My Philtrum

Before I was born,
an angel visited my mother's womb and said,
Forget the cries of sailors, the wailing of strangers
you have heard throughout all your former lives.
You should begin your life as a very empty thing.
Finishing the remarks with *Shh, forget,*
she gently touched my face
and a philtrum formed above my upper lip.

Since being born, I have forgotten
sailors' cries, strangers' wailings,
why I am what I am, why I feel drawn to friends,
and, most of all, why I love her.
Forgotten all of it.
I am what I am,
they are my friends,
she is my lover, all by happenstance.
I believe it all happened by chance.

Since I was born,
beginning by chance and continuing by chance,
I've lived a trivial life.
What must I do to become aware?
Fact: At birth, I'd already surrendered to oblivion.
Fact: The wrinkles on my soul
aren't from age but the sorrow of others.
Fact: Sometimes my philtrum itches
because an angel withdrew her cold finger.
Fact: Every life has cause and effect.
Since birth and until the day I die
I must fight those iron laws.

I don't live by chance.
I don't write by chance.
I don't love by chance.
I can't visualize these facts alone.
I'm always with someone . . .

My friends fall:
One was injured climbing the wall around his ex-lover's house;
another went up a steeple with a comrade, fell, and was hurt.
Their red blood touches my hand, turns into black water
that wets my fingertips.
Suddenly, inspiration enters me.
I scratch my philtrum,
translate their sorrow into words—life from my fingertips.

The woman I love:
three, five, six, nine days . . .
she fills her calendar with days of love,
rushing through morning, past noon, into the afternoon.
She draws out my stretched shadow. Because I love her
death doesn't know who I am;
death, without memory, meaningless,
death that I most fear, I forget about
and scratching my philtrum,
I propose to her for the only time
from past life until the next:
Please stay with me forever.

Questions

I enjoy
questions that are heavy and subtle as coffee at a funeral home:
When I gently caress someone,
will I feel sad if I put myself in that person's place?
If solitude is always ready to welcome you,
is it false solitude?
Although life is composed of volatile moments
why is it so boring as a whole?
Does the body's existence mean the mind has been cleansed
and shrouded alive?
Is my body sick so often because my mind wills it?
If someone opens a drawer and takes something out,
does the drawer feel like it's vomiting?
If I were an object, who would look inside me?
Whenever I go up stairs, why do I think I want to eat them?
Each time I gasp, why do I think I want to stop breathing?
Today has come.
Will tomorrow?
Wind blows:
wind, be outrageous!
If I say that, omitting *wind*, will anyone be outrageous?
Having said that, omitting *revolutions*
will anything revolutionary happen?
And what other questions remain?
What questions, like coffee at a funeral home,
could shape this world to be so heavy and subtle?
And what other questions still puzzle children
and cause their rosy lips to endlessly mumble?

To My Dear Words

Words,
sincere messengers,
you sent a message to my lover, "He loves you,"
and you brought me a hint: "She loves you, too."
Then chortling,
you disappeared, either over the clouds or below my soles.
Following the sound of my love's laughter,
I've lived a life filled with joy.

Words,
names of mothers and fathers,
names of their sons and daughters,
You get old so quickly after birth.
When I look at you I immediately recognize
the names on tombstones.
Chanting the fading names of people I love,
I've lived a life filled with sorrow.

Words,
crumbs of darkness I pick up whenever I pass through shadows,
someday I'll knead the shadow-fragments I've gathered in my life
and shape one huge word.
One word to fit perfectly
into the gap between joy and sorrow.

My old companions,
tonight I'm the least talkative wordsmith on earth.
Sorry, but I'd like to be away from you for a while.
Lying in bed, I'll pose one important question
for tomorrow—that last word will be honored by a kiss,
be a handle with which to raise the soul—
one question that ends with   ?

Days

       We met, uninvited, in the same forest. In spring, we transplanted trees randomly and celebrated the chaos of the season, and in summer we reshaped words into fruit, and the well-rounded silence ripened. In autumn we did our best to escape marriageable age, and in winter we roamed across a snowfield with nonhuman footprints stamped into it like a table of random numbers. Every night we drew out fresh-baked moonlight from one another's crotch and bragged about it. We broke up, an unmarried couple who would never meet again. Time flows on, the words on postcards decrease, and differences between misfortune and fortune fade away. Now we rest like weary mules by the roadside. Except for during our youth, we were unfaithful to our lives. Now the only place we could relax isn't here. We yearn for days spent in a forest that doesn't exist in this world.

Necessary Things

To me six days are necessary—
all except the Sabbath.
Your hand is necessary, of course,
because your palm is a small, mysterious playground.
To chart the crevice of the future,
a very long distance is necessary
because when you're reduced to the size of a dot
for the first time, you seem only a step away.
It's necessary that the past remain a riddle.
That way, only one moment's necessary
for everything to be understood.
At that moment, on the brink of nonexistence,
a vast coastline of thought is necessary.
Words escaped us,
leaving
deep silence during a kiss,
thick darkness within a puddle;
we were not confidants any more…
Occasionally the afternoon brought a monsoon.
Some things were watered and lived
and still other things died.
We were not among them…
The steps that come later are always necessary.
Only the step that comes later is necessary.
Not being that very thing,
not being anything, being anything,
everything...

Good Things

One good thing I did today was
observe a locust dying slowly,
its belly exposed to the sky.
I briefly incarnated its life after death
holding the dead locust, chirring, leaning against a tree.
I wanted to cry, but tears didn't fall,
which was another good thing.
As a gentle brush of light radiating from the sun
caressed my eyes,
the sea's round silhouette was clearly seen.
Then I deliberately recalled only good things
and furtively shoved the scuffed tip of my shoe
into the crevice between thick evening air and solid earth.
Judging by today's good things
perhaps I'm greater than I thought I was.
If I feel delusional, perhaps my heart releases honorable defiance,
grain after grain, into every nook and cranny of my veins.
There are no lucid shadows on this earth:
I shall be moderate in self-confession from now on.
Days of random thoughts continually cross
like crazy quilts beneath my feet.
Life is always full of mystery,
but one day destiny will float in like a blue whale.

Foreigners

This road reminds me of my father's journal—his only literary residue. Occasionally a tiny transparent bird flies up and a tear drops on a piece of paper . . .

My father wrote, "During a trip, you will certainly cry at least once."

I saw three or four blind foreigners on the street and all of them were the same shape and wore the same sunglasses. Maybe they were all identical. No, it's obvious. He was lost and as he wandered up this alley and down that one, he passed me several times. He didn't realize it but I did.

What if I call him "Dad," faking a heartbreaking voice?
Will he flinch in surprise and stop?
Or will he keep walking nonchalantly?
I have been blind about my father
for a long time.
Because he died and is dead
I've been living and am alive.

I'd like to take the blind foreigner by the elbow. When I get him on his way, I'll tell him, "Well, now go this way." And I'll go on my way.

Being a companion isn't about great accomplishments,
I want to repeat constantly.

Not long ago, my friend's rabbi boyfriend left for Israel. Now I'm in Kyoto. "That's a good place for a solo trip," she said, and recommended an art museum in the suburbs. "The architect was I.M. Pei. Isn't that an interesting name?"

When I got there it was closed. Standing in front of its locked doors, I remembered my father's journal. I stood there a long time. I didn't cry. It didn't rain.

During a trip, you'll certainly cry at least once . . .
A bullshit prophecy . . .

Here no one knows
that I secretly pray for hope,
that I am, by nature, an expert on redemption
that my name is
not Pei, or Watanabe, or Thomas,
that at present I'm
a nationless orphan
who has just been abandoned by the past.

I'm in Kyoto now.
And it's snowing.
Along my way
on the shoulders of people going their way, snow falls.
Through black wooden fences that, like italic *I*s,
seem ready to collapse
snowflakes flutter
as a minor god plays like a spoiled child.

The Humor of Exclusion

,

At a motel in Kyoto
I met one of James Joyce's descendants.
When I said *I'm a poet,* he asked,
"Did Kyoto's foreign morning give you inspiration today?
When you're here and can't communicate,
you're excluded at every turn.
When you can't even say, *I'm being excluded,*
can you keep your sense of humor?
Just like me, ha ha!"

Actually, Mr. Joyce was a drunk,
which made me wonder if he came to Kyoto just to drink.
Whenever he saw me — "Let's have a drink together.
Every writer loves to get blathered,
and every great writer is alcoholic."
When I tried to use my deadline as an excuse:
"Fuck the deadline! C'mon! Let's have a drink!"

Actually, Mr. Joyce was bored
Rolling cigarettes and sharing them with me,
he opened up about
how much he hated the noisy Frenchmen in the next room,
how he abhorred the haughty English in his neighbor country
"You know what? Joyce's style
was invented to protest the bastard English language—
Stream of consciousness? Bullshit!"

Actually, Mr. Joyce was a braggart,
boasting that every Joyce in the world was his relative
He recited phrases of James Joyce's poetry
and passages from his own poems.
"This phrase is especially beautiful.

Listen carefully . . .
Pay attention to this spot-on rhyme
Irish blah blah . . . "
I couldn't understand anything at all."

Actually, Mr. Joyce was lonely.
He spoke to me, almost whispering,
"The Humor of Exclusion –
It's the title for your next poem;
write whatever you want with it
You don't need to say I gave it t'you
it's my special gift t'you."
Mr. Joyce threw a wink at me.

Actually, Mr. Joyce was sad
He said quite seriously,
"All dead Irish need two coffins:
One to contain the body
the other to contain the tears;
but, fuck,
one of them is filled too early!"

Actually, there was no way Mr. Joyce could control his anger.
Every night he rode a bicycle out to drink.
I knew when he returned by the sounds
from the verge of the alley:
"Fuck! Fuck! Fuck!"

The one word everyone understands
was the sound of Mr. Joyce majestically returning,
breaking, one by one, the necks of darkness
standing in a row before his eyes.

Open Friendship

The fact is you're just like open air.
I'm not saying this.
You're writing it with your own hand.
You endure,
your transparent hand throbbing endlessly.

After throwing the dice,
I smile at you.
I step toward you
after throwing the dice.

I suddenly see the distant—far distant—future
of this incident,
but I'm really not interested in that.

The fact is you're just like open air.
I'm not confessing.
You're telling me this with your own lips.
You endure,
your transparent lips throbbing ceaselessly.

Perhaps today nothing mystical will happen.
Perhaps tomorrow all shuddering and devotion end.
Perhaps the next day silence becomes God.

It's up to us.
Just as we can laugh at the same time,

everything can end at the same time.
It's up to us.

Wooden Tranquility

I lay my hands on wooden tranquility.
Along its fine grain,
I see, hear, and speak
and then realize delight, the warbling
of eternal delight hidden in the elements of objects.
God, as usual, silently
incubates the golden heart, the sun, in His chest.
Ah, if we could build a house from each
golden crumb that falls from there,
no names would ever be erased
from among glass, fire and stone.
Under the sun that rolls on the edge of the sky
like a shiny bauble of dubious value,
man is an obsessed collector, desperately hoarding
old, faded calligraphies of delight.
Ah, if we'd endured our anxiety a little more,
if God
had helped a little more,
no names would ever disappear
among glass, fire and stone.
I gather my hands and fold them on my chest.
Oblivion erases the fine grain
ever so gently,
lays the dead under wooden tranquility.
Then, to grasp delight, that one delight
that spontaneously crosses over from death,
again I lay my hands upon it.

Good Old Days

That time was good.
Everyone was born poor,
but every single word people spoke
built national prosperity.
Living really meant
the right to randomly say anything.
That time was good.
Even trivial exclamations were marked with silver punctuation,
and absurd metaphors slipped into poetically-metered silk clothes
Uncountable and uncontaminated greatness
made only from words and more words.
Starlight twinkling like a child's curiosity;
a cat sleeping in a circle, posing as a crown,
the distinct meaning of a faint smile,
the thick fragrance of indistinct thinking.
That time was good.
Fierce days eventually
led to peaceful nights
and shattered fragments of the future
that piled today's towers so high, so high.
That time was good.
Falling asleep really meant
that a man listened to another man's whisper
and a man gently closed
another man's tender lids.
That's how that time was.

Theory of Urban Solitude

A cat
lies like a fallen leaf on the road.
A bus like a beast
with a rectangular body and round legs
has stopped in front of it as if in mourning.
Someone says,
Skid marks
mean tires also feel anguish.
Another answers,
Those tires will burst into tears at the last stop.
The new mayor dreams of an enlightened city,
but citizens say the same thing over and over again,
proving that they grow more and more solitary.
Sirens wail faintly in the distance.
Once that sound was a floodlight of terror aimed by a dictator,
but it now sounds sadly nostalgic,
like the scent of gardenias that attract someone blind.
Someone says
Wait and see—
at the last stop, the tires will burst into tears.
Day after day
the difference between friends and the dead disappears,
proving that citizens feel more and more solitary.
Man after man,
cat after cat.

Their Homes

They're cursed
by idealism and materialism at the same time.

In their minds, just before they fall asleep,
a child who never falls asleep
hammers an iron question mark into midnight's feet.
Rancid blood always seeps into their dreams.

And hope is, for them,
just a way to count bread crumbs in their pockets.
They never get an accurate count
because more crumble as they count,
and yet they can't stop counting!

Inequality is
the gap between
those who pose countless questions but get no proper answers
and those who pose no proper questions but get countless answers

They endlessly wander the streets.
To call them back into their homes,
we must break all the windows facing the street.

Their homes have no doors
Their homes are inflammable.

This is their tragedy.
We must protect their homes.

If There 's Just One Flat Stone

January 20, 2011: the Second Anniversary of the Yongsan Tragedy

There's nothing here now,
as if from the beginning there was nothing here.
Nothing is here.
This place is empty.
It's turned into a wasteland,
and at the seven o'clock evening service
the faint moonlight that once lowered Jacob's ladder to the roof
now slavishly prostrates itself on the ground
only to flatter the luster of expensive cars.
We're stunned that nothing is here.

If there's just one flat stone,
we'll sit on it and look back
at the demolished building, floor by floor,
at broken windows, piece by piece,
at mashed tiles, shard by shard.
Proof of slaughter,
charred by the inferno, stained with blood and strips of flesh.
Days after the slaughter:
petitions, protests, prayers.

If there's just one flat stone,
we'll sit on it and reminisce about
baseball and fishing in our youth,
Bible verses that struck the old in their hearts,
numerous grievances and humble dreams.
Then we'll talk about why we had to occupy Yongsan.
We shall not be coerced again!
This time we shall fight, shall try to win!
We'll talk about the reckless obligation that, on that day,
suddenly flowed out of one soul and into others.

If there's just one flat stone
we'll sit on it and ask each other,
What will the butchers think of next?
They strangled us before we even wailed,
they built our coffins even before we died—
before we had the chance to prove our innocence.
These passersby pretending to be citizens
who scurried past, casting cold glances.
Where on earth were they going?

If there's just one flat stone
we shall not just sit.
We'll stand on it and conjure
the human beings, all of them,
each one a watchtower among the flames
hanging on the steep edge of survival
and swaying between trash and ash.
These souls can do nothing but scream,
People are here!
Please, people are here!

If there's just one flat stone
we'll stand on it, put our heads together, and examine
a destiny coiled toward misfortune like rusty barbed wire,
lives that tumble   toward misery like small pebbles.
We'll be absorbed in the cause, the root of everything.
And when there's no way to find the answer,
we who are ignorant shall shout,
We won't live like this anymore!
We who are nice shall plead,
Why do you make us hate you? We don't deserve this pain!

If there's just one flat stone
we'll do our best to bring as many souls
as possible onto it.
Mouths that are always hungry.
Mouths so obsessed with eating.
When the tattered lips are piled up
and a miraculously high steeple of echoes is raised,
we shall no longer be afraid to tell
the truth that no one wanted to hear,
the truth swirling and spewing from our throats.
So if we stand on a flat stone,
we should talk about hope, only hope:
The living and the dead.
The happy and the sad.
The evil and the good.
Each of us must decide.

A Flower Falls

Autumn has arrived on earth.
Strange light, never seen before, is softly
pressing everyone's feet.
At this moment, a flower falls,
someone moves toward something,
someone else falls,
something goes wrong.
Orphans, though still human, can't tell
family from neighbors,
good people from bad,
so they yearn for anyone.
A flower falls.
Wandering in time, whirling around
the earlobe of a brief moment,
a gaze someone hurriedly withdraws,
a finger sadly pointing at something.
A weary key
that fits no earthly door
hovers idly, forever, in the air.

A Boy Answers His Own Question

Boy, you hurl a question.
Enormous curiosity
picks up your fingertip and points it at the universe.
Cross this forest
and on the other side I'll give you an iron answer,
but the person who answers isn't wise.
A faraway star,
a fluttering flag,
lips with no hostility,
unknown influences cast upon your life.
Boy, you may fall before you reach the other side of the forest.
Then you'll be finished
and an old man will begin.
Chaos then calamity,
calamity then crushing disillusionment.
Boy, aren't you afraid?
Civilization will begin to rustle
like dead fathers' wills.
Boy, you hurl a question
that is the crumb of a bigger question.
Cross this forest
and on the other side I'll give you a fireball answer,
but it won't be the gift you expect.
It will only be one sentence.
Read that sentence.
Then, boy, you
will never remember death.

A Stone Which Isn't Dazzling

From now on we'll write
words that are excessive, abundant
words with shape and color,
as if we prepare a gift,
as if we load our guns.
Words and sentences
that are right as well as wrong,
beautiful as well as anguished,
from a far place to a farther place,
passing through you for you.
Something absolute
that no lover nor king nor god
could give me,
your finger
will point on their behalf.
So we must write—
lifting to eye level
the stone rolling at our feet,
a stone which isn't dazzling—
until it trembles.

Creation

My shadow is a different person with your name.
Once we all were babies, born stones
heated by flame.
It's said our steps gradually evolved
into simpler motions so we wouldn't fall,
but that doesn't matter. Let's ignore it,
because the subtlest step is freedom.

Betraying our poor ancestors, we
manage to establish our own poverty,
our own chaos and faith.
Novel poverty pervades the night.
Moonlight licks the poison-stained edges
and is torn into hundreds and hundreds of shreds.

We're insignificant slaves on an immense planet.
We fail at things that should not be failures,
repeat things that should not be repeated.
Thus, when earth's final winter comes,
we'll carefully peel this shining glass marble to feed ourselves
as we look at one another with bloodshot eyes.

We meet inside words shaped by delusion
and scream at the world's abyss.
Now is the time most worthy
of being called creation.
Like a drop of ink dissipates in flowing rainwater,
the impossible inscription is about to begin.

Here Now

I accidentally visited life.
When I die, I'll return to be brother to the dogs
be like those silent and stiff four-footed animals,
without conscience, without soul.
But I'm here now
with human brothers.
I feel good because
as I read a thick book titled *Life,*
composed of millions and millions of warm bare feet,
thump thump thump
ruddy footprints are stamped in my eyes.
Following the sound of coughing and guitars,
which has been heard since before I was born,
I came upon human beings
who are said to carry hearts like stars in bright daylight.
By the way, for a moment . . . let me pose a question:
What's the shortest distance between two hearts?
A straight line? No!
Two people inevitably,
inevitably embrace.
The mathematics of love shifts the Archimedean point
from space to a navel,
conceives two hearts in one chest,
builds a vast constellation with only two stars.
How many shapes God joined together
to assemble the human soul!
So I'm here now
to be human,
to love,
to stay a very short time at a humble whistle stop
on the way from nothingness to nothingness.

The Soul Between Two Trees

The one who controls me is not the one who cares for me
but someone who makes me feel alone, someone
who looks at me as if looking into the distance,
someone who casts my soul as far away as possible,
to a place where the stain of my sin is too tiny to be seen.

There are two of me:
One is a sinner,
the other has no words.
Between birth and death,
I'm not able to say
the things I should say.
It's my own fault that I'm silent.
I know it's bad and sad.

With a timid sigh
I whisper, *Where is my guardian angel?*
Perhaps when I was born, an angel shouted "Hurrah!"
then choked on a cloud, and fell.
Bad luck isn't being alive at noon
and dead by midnight.

During life I scatter my bits of my soul here and there,
on every side of night, in all the corners of day
lest anyone should rake them
into a pile again.
At times, I pass between two trees
and each time, someone shouts at me,
He-e-e-y-y, stop for a moment!
Right there, I want you to stay right there!

It's my own fault that I'm silent.
I know it's bad and sad.
I know, too, that the soul
is only visible for a moment,
like a bird flying between two trees.

A Heart Gives Birth to a Future

My heart has throbbed
exactly 1.5 billion times until this moment.
To celebrate, I give a big yawn.
My life is so boring,
I've counted each heartbeat since my birth.

While turning pages, sleepy-eyed,
I burned my hand on the hottest page.
What's written there?
Words that quote a firebrand.
Who's the author?
Perhaps Prometheus' descendant.
The dream that forged the corners of the book
still sears my fingers.

I close the book and look outside.
Days have always been waiting in time
but could never become a future—
fourteen thousand, nine hundred and ninety-eight days thus far.
My life is so boring
I've counted each day since my birth.

Spring days, when a branch forms a green cross with another
          branch,
a flower whispers secret flower language to another flower,
a person gives another person an immortal shoulder.
When will such spring days come?

At the right time, a beautiful woman turns a street corner.
Like an emissary of the people,
she comes toward me, a flaming book in her hand.
When she reaches me, I'll embrace her!

And the crowds massed behind her, arms opened wide!!

From now on, I don't have to count my heartbeats.
Each time my heart leaps,
one monumental future is born.

First Line

I'm longing for a first line.
Once it's written,
I'll be happy as when watching the first snow.
From the round silence
that holds the phantom pregnancy of future enthusiasm,
the first line will be delivered.
The first line of a love letter,
the first line of a manifesto,
the first line of ice
that no fire can thaw.
Once it's written,
I'll be as happy as at the birth of my first child.
Once it's written,
only half of me will wrestle with death.
The other half
will form a wreath of fire
that no ice can cool.

Part II

None of the World's Business

Breaking up with you is none of the world's business.
I'm waiting for the apocalypse ...
We'll break up after that.
When is the apocalypse?

Ad Mundi (To the World).

World
I'm gonna tell you, as a foreigner who abandoned his home,
how blessed I am that at least I still breathe.
After a huge shadow passed above my head,
I deliberately denied the darkness of the cloud.
I'm gonna tell you, my transcendental inspiration
is at a transcendent moment.

World
I hate the world to death, but that means
I love the world oh so much as well.
I have no right to pass judgment on the affairs of the world.
If I'd been qualified for that, my father
wouldn't have closed his eyes
in such solitude, wouldn't have left such a great child behind.
Although he died in his own home, wasn't his death still tragic?
Didn't I wail? Didn't my mother wail even louder?
Since that day, haven't our lives been agony?
Living. Living today and living tomorrow.
The days of our lives are like that, aren't they?

World
if I'd been more prudent and disciplined,
I could have ruled the small country destiny might have given me
surrounded by constellations, ramparts, maidens all bowing to me
in front of my small court.
I would have shouted, *God is distant*, then lifted my finger
to point at the ash-gray corner of the heavens where God lazily
reclines beyond the darkness.
To prove my accusation came from a hardened heart,
and beyond that, from my divine soul,
I would have trampled a touch-me-not that just opened at my feet

as if it were God's tiny fist.
Then, going beyond arrogance, as the first signal to proceed into
deep nonexistence,
I would have burst into gales of laughter.

World,
I can't do that.
As a very discouraged foreigner who has no home,
I'll beg for just a wisp of warm breath,
touch my frozen finger to your lips.
I'll say, sobbing:
In winter many people will die.
Whether home or away, they'll die.
Whether rich or poor, they'll die.
Neighbors will disappear
without a trace, like insignificant dust,
no matter how discreetly and gently I greet them
when my eyes meet theirs on the street.
It's totally useless; on a horribly cold winter night
fragile people like my father are going to die.

World
when I talk to you, I passionately want to hold you.
When I hold you, from the swaying thickets of memory
swarms of butterflies are resurrected and rise.
With a simple gesture, you shine on the cheekbones of every boy,
you ring morning bells to open my eyes.
At dusk, your two suns fill my world with the colors of sunset.
At night, you transform sperm from my testicles into hundreds
of thousands of twinkling fireflies.
And, finally in my bed,
telling me a story about a brave wolf, no ordinary dog,

you give me pleasure in my exhaustion so
I passionately want to hold you and fall asleep.

World
I'm gonna tell you, as a foreigner who abandoned his home,
my words will not praise nor scream about the human condition.
They'll be trivial and light
like beads of sweat falling from an ill and sensitive boy's forehead
onto the rocky path he trudges, his back to the setting sun.
When I finish speaking and turn my back to you,
I'll be absorbed into a silence vast as an abyss
and a solitude deep as the shadow of a giant whale.
And into a future that has no connection with any worldly plan,
into empty hours with only the promise of desperation,
I'll walk like a sad and naked animal.
So please, hear this stranger out.

World
I have no idea
where you are now.
Does your forehead soar toward the meridian?
Do your shoulders stretch toward the ocean?
Are your eyes 2 a.m.?
Are your lips 3 a.m.?
Between the hot, moist parts of your body,
do numerous cities rise and fall all in a single night?
Your body is heartbreaking, like a civilization far, far beyond reach.
World,
the one who'll listen to this pathetic, worthless stranger's words,
my world of worlds,
the home to which I shall eventually return
where, indeed, are you now?

The Word "Me"

I don't like the word "me" very much.
As if it's the only available option,
I've bet on "me" so many times.
Yet very rarely do I like the word.
At night, when I say "me" while in bed
the word seems as distant as the horizon
no, even farther, beyond the horizon: the hometown I left behind.
I like "me" better when it's on the ground instead of in the air.
Yesterday when I took a walk I found a "me"
someone had scratched into the dirt path with a twig.
How lonely was the person who wrote that word?
Maybe "me" was written on the ground
while remembering a hometown left behind
or gazing at a horizon that would be approached alone.
I suddenly felt I needed to protect that word
so I surrounded it with pebbles I'd selected.
Of course, in less than a day, by rain or wind
or by a nonchalant kick, the word will vanish without a trace.
I like "me" better when it's intaglio rather than carved in relief.
Writing the word is accepting its disappearance as fate.
I coddle it like the baby I never birthed.
But I worship the word "me" the most
when the word passes through your ear,
circulates through your entire body,
and returns through your lips as the word "you."
I know that, without you,
each time I say "me"
I descend dark stone steps, one by one, toward nothingness.
But today, smiling at me
you told me a story that began, "This is you…"
The story made no mention of horizon or hometown
but I knew. Tonight I'm

going to fall slowly into a sleep more peaceful than death,
constantly repeating *This is me. . . This is me. . .*
as if it is the only gift I was ever given.

Fascination

When two people are in love
there's always a silent third between them
who leads them into the ethereal
because in love there must be an angel for only two.
When one of the two disappears,
the angel draws near the one in sorrow
because in love there must
be an angel to whisper *Don't forget.*

But I don't know
the exact moment when God severs day and night,
the exact moment when, without God's awareness, two people
hurriedly trade souls.

That time can be called fascination.

Following fascination,
time flies like an arrow.

Following fascination,
expressions are shaped by someone always in the corner of the eye.

Following fascination,
expressions are eternally due to someone always in the corner of
        the eye.

So there's no choice but to pile love and secrets
carefully, with utmost attention, throughout life,
just as putting "Black Stone on a White Stone."

I vaguely remember
water beading on a woman's shoulder as she finished her

shower
scattering into more, smaller beads
just before the man found the courage to wipe them off,
a beam of dim light flowing between curtains,
a scrap of darkness held between their lips.

By the way,
were the beginning and the end both inside one eye?

Now I remember everything:
numerous expressions woven in the eyes
connected to each other like a spider's web;
the never-ending story continuing until dawn
like a hungry spider pacing his web;
a bright and unfamiliar world
that on that day lost a word for "morning"
which had been preserved since ancient days.

Bird

We make love
without knowing what we want,
surrounded by very bright or very dark air.

When we make love,
I whisper in your ear, glistening in silver-grey moonlight,
What are you afraid of now?
What are you thinking about now?

I love you. I confess to you three times.
Tee-hee-hee. Laughter rolls from your lips like falling pebbles.
A wisp of breeze that just brushed my face
will soon caress your face with completely different hands.

We met. We met several times.
Several times more, we made love,
love composed of ordinary emotions and humble desires.

I know. If we owned a bird
we'd very sadly
let it out the window this evening.
Then we'd giggle together.
Tee-hee-hee. With that strange image, we make love.

When we make love, we play with each other's soul as if with
round pebbles.
But how can this happen
when we're so disgusted with our individual souls?

When love-making is finished, finished, your hands will be moist
as the skin of a newborn baby that has yet to absorb its handful
of spirit. When I clasp your hands, I feel

your hands gradually grow thinner in my hands,
just like a small bird I've never owned.

You'll fly away.
Don't fly away.
You'll fly away.

You Hear with Ears of Corn

I moved forward anticipating the moment of fascination.
Love was elaborately planned.
In a dream filled with reconciliation and affection,
you asked,
A cornfield has so many ears,
how can it tolerate the noise of the wind?
Your innocence
was majestic within the boundary of clouds.
Love is good because it exaggerates life.
With your face absorbed by the classic enigma,
you fell asleep,
and stupid, stupid me
visualized tomorrow's inevitable and catastrophic end.
I gambled that you'd cry
before I would;
on whether it would be breakup or reunion.
When you woke you said, *In my dream*
I was a field of corn and you were the wind
I heard you singing with a thousand
ears of corn.
I was the first one who cried.
I'll see you again in the next life.

Sleeping Late

Stars delicately adapt to darkness.
They calmly gaze into facets of night that were polished by time.
We return home, walking on damp soil,
stamping footprints that smell like well-ripened apples.

In which of my ears do more whispers puddle?
The one opposite the side on which I, curled up, sleep.
The pit where your dry breath drops.

Crystals of dawn, shifting from lips to dew.
Your hands have never counted gold coins.
They always give me the wrong key to morning's lock.

Behind me, you ask in a low voice
What time is it now?

I contemplate
a path that connects two far-apart eyes,
the trembling needle of a rusty compass.

Ten a.m.
You say, *Time to get up.*

The Lost Gift

Breaking up is a sign from different stars
to we who are dying day by day,
but I won't accept that it's over
until trustworthy death finally comes.
The strange gift you gave me,
so frightening in this world
may be comforting in the next.
How can I describe it?
It's lost.
It was nameless and pitiful.
A meteorite that fell insignificantly one night,
a clock that stopped ten years ago,
a shoulder where my hand rested briefly then dropped away:
There was a time when I heard things take a long, deep breath
as they imploded in the external world.
There was a time when I listened and wept.

Star

A star is twinkling

in Latin in the Northern Hemisphere,
in Maori in the Southern Hemisphere.

A star is twinkling: that star

is my father, about whom my mother reminisces.

She simply gazes,
gazes...

Dad's Tale: Red Mountain and Rabbits

When Dad was young he raised rabbits on a red mountain.
They'll multiply from ten to a hundred, a hundred to a thousand!
he shouted, shaking his fists at the world below.
Dad raised rabbits, reading Hemingway and Steinbeck.
Amateur astrologist, he interpreted the signs in flickering stars
and in the moon's halo,
gulped down wild grape wine he brewed himself,
lifted a dry twig and scrawled elusive letters in the air.
And when Dad got drunk, he'd bleakly state that
his solitary madness was multiplying as fast as the rabbits.

But day by day, Dad's shouts got rusty and his fists cracked.
His enlightenment was aimless, his courage slouched.
One day, conservation officers raided his rabbit farm.
He rushed to the village below the mountain
and asked for help from Mom, a pretty bookkeeper
in a piece goods shop.
Dad cried, recalling the cute, lovable rabbits he'd left behind
          on the mountain.
Her long fingers caressed his scraggly hair
as her free hand clicked the abacus beads.
When Dad was drunk he recalled that time and said,
Your mother was a rare girl, possessing both sympathy and common sense.

Time flowed and three rabbit-like children were born to them.
Dad's solitude and madness gradually ebbed.
To be the breadwinner, Dad passed the civil servants' exam
and raised the three of us, reading Hemingway and Steinbeck.
Dad sometimes wrote and sometimes talked,
wrote and talked: sometimes disillusionment, sometimes shame
as if that were the only way to find satisfaction.

When Dad was drunk and drowning in remorse, he'd say,
I was the owner of a promising rabbit farm,
I was smart enough to pass the civil servants' exam
on my first attempt,
but those cunning officers ruthlessly butchered my rabbits —
Now I've become a civil servant, just like those bastards.
For damn money I've become the enemy!
One day, I will go back to the red mountain.
Maybe some rabbits survived and are waiting for me there...

Dad raised rabbits on a red mountain
Dad raised all three of us below the mountain.
Desire, wearing a rusty crown, wandered through his mind.
He couldn't love anyone, but he also couldn't hate.
He and the sun were dying together, in hot, eternal, passion...

Dad passed away one summer day a few years ago.

I don't know which red mountain was Dad's.
I don't even know if his story was true.
No matter where it is, whether real or not,
Dad has finally returned to his red mountain,
to the red mountain where his cute, lovable rabbits still live,
to the space where solitude and insanity still burn.

Nostalgia

Materialists die early.
They evangelize paradox,
are arsonists who throw flames into their own souls.
A judge wrestles with the questions:
Is remorse evidence of conscience?
Evidence of guilt?
The law accepts
cold, hard physical evidence,
but a minstrel sings
of a wide cliff on which mellow mosses flourish,
of the life of an antelope,
of being born and dying between yawn and yawn,
of enough oblivion to fill a stomach
and be regurgitated throughout life,
of the perpetual sound of dry-heaving
heard from beyond the law of memory.
I won't look back.
Even though I'm alive
I'm not really living.

Speaking Strangely

Sitting alone on a park bench,
I read the time on my watch.
I fathom silence spreading between the hands
and violence ticking beneath that.
In the afternoon, split precisely halfway between light and dark,
like a growing child,
like a dying bird,
I strangely speak.
During my walk I banished random thoughts
and buried my left hand in a pile of leaves by the path.
It will be weird if I say
that hand died before I did.
When I kissed her,
her head raised and inflated.
Her mouth infused a fragrant whistle into mine.
I thought
Maybe her mind will sweep me into an enchantment.
Sitting alone on a park bench,
I gaze at my gradually fading shadow.
It will be sad if I say
my shadow was darker than yours.
I finally drop my head,
not because I'm sad
but because, in my head, a flower fell.
This is the afternoon when all flowers in my head wither,
the afternoon when I murmur strange words
sitting alone on a park bench.
Looking at my watch, I wonder what time it is.
It is precisely halfway between silence and violence.

Dream about a Fig

I want some figs,
you told me then.
It was the middle of winter.
After wandering the night streets
I found some dried figs.

You said,
Ho ho ho, good job.
Ho ho ho, I'm sure dried figs are the same figs as fresh.
You enthusiastically ate one of them.
I said,
I'm allergic to figs
I can't breathe after even one bite.

You said,
Ho ho ho, you sound silly,
and fell asleep peacefully
hugging your old dog.

Sometimes I wonder
if your old dog died.
Sometimes I hear about you.
People say you became a celebrity
who attends celebrity funerals,
that you became even more beautiful.

Sometimes I'm curious
about when your beauty will end,
about what age you'll die.

I had a dream about you yesterday.
We shared a fig.

Then you fell asleep, peacefully
hugging your old dog.
Lying next to you, I couldn't breathe.
I closed my eyes, shed tears,
and finally died.

Lunar Calendar

When I was just so sad
I discovered an ash-gray pebble beneath my feet.
At that time I barely remembered my name
and told myself
tomorrow I'll feel all right.
Tomorrow, in the lunar calendar,
everything in the past is forgotten.

When I was young, some of my journeys
were toward the west,
simply "west"
rather than a specific destination.
At that time, I sang:
A man who stood on a rock yesterday
is lying beneath a rock today.
A man who lay beneath a rock yesterday
has become a rock beside a rock today.

When I was just so sad,
I read the horizon to the west
in as much of an undertone as possible.
In the lunar calendar, the west is east of yesterday
and a horizon is a perfect three-dimensional shape.
At that time, I'd forgotten my name
and was sluggishly expanding
the area in which my destiny would spread in the future
like meteor pockmarks on the dark side of the moon.

When I was just so sad
I discovered an ash-gray pebble beneath my feet.
In the lunar calendar, that
was a human's unhealed scab,

and at that time your lovely name,
already halfway erased on earth,
glowed, phosphorescent blue, like a fossil.

Time of Transformation

Without hesitation, life started.
As little sprigs
were dying between one season and the next,
I furrowed my brow and transplanted
their feeble bodies there.
Each night, a burnt offering
as I placed flowers, incense and candles upon time's grave,
burning the memories of a hundred days.
After becoming an adult,
I got old, but despite getting old,
I didn't want to die.
All my wanderings were useless,
my journeys were worthless.
The oceans' waves were a musical score,
the crying of the clouds couldn't shake any shadows.
Otherwise, I would never have returned.
I can never stay,
nor can I ever disappear.
Long ago I met a sage on the street who said,
Indonesia has fourteen thousand islands and
each of them has its own volcano.
Do you cherish
the secret that propels you toward the apocalypse?
Today I remembered what he said so long ago
and I secretly had to retract a foolish decision made
while watching your white face as you put rice in your mouth.
You've fallen asleep beside me, like a child.
Watching you sleep,
I inch from human silence
toward the silence of a worm.
I have no doubt that's the most desirable path
toward the apocalypse.

A Snob's Room

He lives in a room without curves.
He thinks this room
is a place of exile, clipped in precise angles.
Looking at the empty cage hanging from the ceiling,
he thinks,
A birdcage with no bird—
isn't that just perfect?
He's become addicted to coffee and cigarettes here
and desirable personality traits.
Recalling waves on a pebbled beach
which he heard with someone long ago,
the serenade corresponds well with this evening.
He falls into a good feeling.
He lives in a room without curves
as if, while leaving, someone erased
all of the curves.
He thinks good taste is
something like a female pedigreed cat
which will neither stay nor flee.
Elegance. He's fascinated
by elegance and is sure
his unhappiness
has some positive points,
is sure that, in this empty room, he is now
creating one perfect attitude.

Granada

Tying loose wind to my feet,
throwing a firm attitude around my shoulders,
I leave on a journey.
Don't leave,
the fireballs pleaded with my eyes.
I have no companion for this journey.
Although we'd been together a long time,
my attitude was firmer than at any other time.
Suh swah suh swah.
My feet move forward, dragging the wind.
The sound of the noon bell falls at my feet.
One, two, three . . .
A kingdom lasts longer than a king.
Alhambra lasts longer than a kingdom.
cypress wood lasts longer than Alhambra.
Here death
snatches the transparent laurel wreath from life
and forcefully throws it down on the cold stone path.
Time has flowed so long,
but despite moving forward, there's nothing to be found.
I've become an old man
and feel so lonely.
I long for the companion who was with me until yesterday.
I long for the dark-skinned woman who hid fire in her eyes.
I leave on a journey,
tying loose wind to my feet,
throwing a firm attitude around my shoulders.
I have to leave
even if I collapse on the path with my first step.
The sound of the noon bell falls at my feet
one, two, three . . .
even if a fourth sound is never heard.

Spending the Night Alone in a Motel

I gaze into an evening ocean branded with clouds.
Waves from my unsalvageable wreck swell toward another wreck.
How can I forget you?
You—scattered among such trivial memories.

When I turn off the lights and close the book,
the darkness is complete.
Reading between the lines, my sidelong glance traces moonlight
that immediately permeates the room.

I passionately wish to hug myself
and want to build a towering snowman on that sandy beach
and make it trample this world in just two steps.
Sometimes, in my mind,
a clothed man and a naked man
discuss the list of people who abandoned me.
Other deaths occur to me sporadically.

Winter nights full of regret and self-scorn,
a beast gnashing its teeth at the past.
A fierce phantasm from the future splitting the waves,
growing taller and taller above the horizon.
At that time, the soul, like from a roiling kettle,
is born before I can even count to three,
born not from perfect chaos but from chaotic perfection.

From the fridge in the corner of the motel room
a thread of light leaks out and begins to break the world into bits.

Will I make an irreparable decision? Will I?

Contemplation

In a climate that has no weather
I gaze into the horizon;
I already know
a shadow is evidence
that the sun is eternally scrutinizing an object.

No one is near me now.
In my head is simply one meek lamb
whose legs are evaporating,
whose head is evaporating,
whose tail is evaporating.
It has become an oval cloud
It has become pure.

In my dream, I fall into danger little by little
and scream regularly.
I wish
I could follow the attitude of a simple fisherman
who isn't too absorbed in thought.
My ears would gather the soft sound of water ripples one by one,
my eyes would stroke the blunt horn tip of moonlight.
Little by little, I'd feel safe,
would regularly cherish hope.

I wake up at the crack of dawn beneath a net of air,
as if last night's dream were a fish I luckily caught.
My heart flutters in my chest
as I gaze into the horizon—
the widest object in the world.
After a wait I didn't want,
I suddenly realize
that a clock proves time is a lie.

I have a hunch that something
might be a great miracle.
No matter what it is,
I'll contemplate it
for a long, long time.

April

I was longing for news from you
one spring day when my fingers reached out the window
and caressed unknown starlight,
the rusty steeple of an imperial building,
a magnolia branch brimming with buds.

I was longing for news from you
one spring day when my fingers caressed nothing but fingers.

News from you came in April.
News from you came like skipping stones
in the silence between January and March.
In April, news from you came for the last time.

In May, I longed for more news from you.
In June, an angel dropped by my room to comfort me
and left, shaking her head, *I'd rather be a devil.*
When the psychologist asked, "How are you feeling today?"
I knitted my brows
and she wrote very disturbing sentences in her notebook.

I was . . . news from you . . .
Of course, still in July . . .
News from you came in April.
In April, news from you came for the last time.

In August wings sprouted from my shoulders,
in September they were big as an oak, so at night I fell asleep
beneath them.
In October I jumped from the roof and soared.
In November I passed Mars and Jupiter and reached Saturn.

As I squatted on the porch of the cosmos and gazed at distant
        earth
my shoes, which I had carefully removed, waited for me
like an old dog lying on its belly.
In December, I returned
bringing a hot winter that wasn't on the calendar.

News from you came in April
April was the last month of that year
and the first month of the next.

I longed for news from you
and waited for a very long time.

The Gravity of Destiny

My eyes can't look into the sun for very long,
but everyone
has eyes strong enough to change the shape of the sky.

During the entire walk, a dog barked without a break
at passersby and cars,
at trees and steeples,
even at clouds and the blue sky beyond.

What a ruckus!
Passersby, cars, trees, steeples, clouds, blue sky:
he must be scared of every single thing.
In this world, what wouldn't be frightening?

What if you had the power to change your destiny?

The dog ahead of me stops barking and turns around.
When the gravity between the dog and me prickles my eyes,
I smile and the dog wags its tail.

I recall my love
giggling and showing the white teeth of a distant star
whenever I turned around with a thirst for salvation.

Things belonging to my destiny;
things not belonging to my destiny.
My mischievous love secretly
hides a ticklish gravity between the two.

What if I have the power to change my destiny . . . ?

I do.

Letter to H.A.

I accidentally saw your writing; fascinating writing that made me instantly fall in love with you. Were you writing about the soul? I believe all the writing in the world is about the soul. You and I have run into each other in the library and in a bookstore, but even when we were closest to each other, our shadows never overlapped. Now, the distance between us is the greatest it's ever been. This is a foreign city with a weird name that means *land where starlight pecks at the expressions in people's eyes as fat chicken feed.* Morning in this poor country is a great accomplishment, just as in any other place: lifting the sun to the highest spot in the sky by noon. What did your soul's morning lift to its highest spot? It's rained since dawn. Sometimes I believe it rains in the name of the Father, the Son, and the Holy Ghost. Leaves fall in the order of how little faith they have. However, it's important to remember that true believers also face a catastrophic end. Just as it happened to you. I believe in God, like you did. Contemplating the impossible is my hobby. So do you understand now why I'm writing a letter to you? You died a long time ago. Your body perished; no traces remain. There's no way that any mixed-race child, cat, or begonia can be raised by us. Should I convince myself it's a blessing that we can't kiss? Now, looking at a black and white photograph of you with a cigarette between your lips, I put a cigarette between my lips. I'm going to light this cigarette with the flame of the candle that constantly emits an unfamiliar scent above the table, and then, with that same flame, burn this letter after I've written the last sentence. I believe that's the only way for this letter to reach you.

Stephen Haggard's Death

It's been a while since the fighting ended,
yet he still thinks about death today.
Of course, not for too long.
Not too deeply
but with an actor's extravagantly exaggerated gestures,
like a slightly immature critic speaks.
Come on, everyone, come down from your futile plans and lie down here.
I'll tell you about death. And then . . .
Ah, ah, I feel so tired. How about continuing this tomorrow?
Like that.
During a brief silence, his weary tongue
tenderly embraces sounds from different songs and falls into a
short nap.

It's been a while since the fighting ended
yet today he's still on a mission.
With feet that don't feel ticklish any more when tickled,
not by ship but by train,
not from Wales to Scotland
but from Cairo to Palestine,
under shabby dark clouds shredded by a worm-like blueness
he thinks while resting:
Visit every poor village equally,
keeep your focus on death
traveling is the gentlest strife.
He marks the darkness by dipping a dry foxtail into a drop of
wind.

In the train's window, he watches the reflection of his face
change strangely into dry, hard dough.
Ah, ah, where the hell is this?
In deep grief induced by his mask of grief

he talks to himself:
My sole reader
I'll tell you about death, no matter where this is.
You have to let go of your futile plans.
You have to ride the precarious rope of life.
As one tear drops
he talks to himself once more:
My war is over. My war is over.
I have nothing left to say.
There are no more acting roles for me.

Under the night sky where shooting stars draw slender slashes
            in the air
fatigued with hunger, he writes:
Yesterday I stood for a long time in front of a bakery window
with the sign CLOSED TODAY *hanging on it.*
Sipping kudzu tea that has long grown cool,
he ruminates over his short life,
 spent wandering from one country to another.
For the first time in a long time, he says *death* in proper British
            pronunciation.
Ah, ah, how familiar and cozy.
In fact, since his birth, the letters of death
—d-e-a-t-h — have been jumbled in his name.

Anyway, his war is over.
Another tear drops;
he hurriedly erases the sentence he just wrote,
and without delay aims the pistol at his head
and pulls the trigger.
Not on a ship but on a train,
not from Wales to Scotland,

but on the way from Cairo to Palestine,
the temple has been penetrated by the bullet.

That's how his war ended.
No matter how hard he tries,
he won't be able to complete a thick report on the battle.
He won't be able to write one single line of a poem of death.
Even the miserable truth
won't inspire him anymore.

An Obscure Author

As I awakened from deep sleep,
a bell broke,
a string snapped,
a pen flew out of nowhere and stabbed me in the heart
I don't know where the dead are piled in the open fields
(maybe geniuses know),
I've never seen human nature delicately carved in the heavens
(maybe geniuses have).
But I don't care;
I won't write carelessly.
This winter I'll swiftly complete my first masterpiece,
but there will be no written dedication.
Instead I'll dedicate it to
all the readers
and respectful critics
who don't even know who I am

Chronology

I like poetry better than fiction.
I like the chronology of a writer's life more than a poem
because I'm always fascinated by the side closest to the grave.
When fish die, they sink into the abyss
and become arrows (>----▷) that point to each other's deaths,
so I like them.
A fish's skeleton's head and eye are the end of the chronology of a
fish's life.
I fall into an abyss of random thoughts
My fists swell like an octopus head in the abyss and burst,
squirting black ink instead of blood into the water,
but not even ink
wants to return to the world of the Dark Ages.
Spirals of random thought have no end.
No one can grab me.
The cosmos is my collar.
No one can laugh at me.
The chronology of my life is billions of light years
and coming at full speed from eternity
toward my humble grave, yet to be dug,
toward brilliant earth where my grave has yet to be dug.

Love Is My Weakness

You read a gay activist's poem to me,
a poem that is powerful, beautiful, and mystical.
A poem where a world of sorrow my language can never reach
spreads vividly, like a constellation across the night sky.
I feel pain.
Half from jealousy, half from inspiration.
But I listen, just nodding my head. For the first time
in a really long time
I've become a meek reader
who knows how to listen to a sincere voice.

When you finished reading, you said with a smile:
If you were gay
you could write a poem as good as this.
Loving me is your only weakness.
Maybe you didn't mean it,
but under your good intentions and wit
hides a very sharp message.
I'm a straight, middle-class poet.
That isn't my only weakness
but it's the limit of my true nature, isn't it?

Today I got two phone calls.
One said:
Congratulations! Your poem has been selected as "Poem of the Year."
Please send us your acceptance speech by tomorrow.
The other one said:
Sorry, but your poem is too complicated to read at our public rally.
Would you send us a revision that is easier to express by tomorrow?
These two people were talking about the same poem.
I must obey each one. By tomorrow
I should send a formal, literary acceptance speech

as well as an appropriate revision. Since I'm a sincere poet
as well as a good citizen, they expect this from me.

By the way, there's something I didn't tell you:
I proposed to you in my poem.
Phfffff, I blew a wisp of warm breath into your ear;
you accepted with a bright smile that said *Yes!*
I'm thinking I'll propose to you someday
in extremely common and direct language,
so to speak, not poetic at all,
in language with no more than two sentences.
I know those two sentences, though not at all poetic,
will determine the happiness in of my life.

One more thing I didn't tell you:
while you were reading the poem, I happened to
see an old man walking past the window.
As he walked so slowly under the fragrant snowbell tree,
weirdly shuffling his feet,
he made a path through the exquisite embroidery of the fallen
flowers.
His eyes met mine.
No. Actually they didn't.
The old man was just an image,
an ash-gray leather sack cast from a world I can't speak for.
If the old man's eyes had met mine
for only one second, I would have written like this:

He seemed to say to me:
Poet, sing!
Not about my upcoming death,
which anyone can foresee,

but about what no one knows, my life.
Sing about my sad love and painful frustration.
Sing about how I never gave up hope.
Sing about how I overcame it all and survived, and how today
my eyes accidentally met yours under a fragrant snowbell tree.
Although I'm carrying so many memories on my shoulders,
why doesn't any single melody flow inside them?
Poet, standing by the window
sing about me. Please sing a song that says my weary shadow
has a peculiar strength that other shadows don't.

When you'd finished reading the poem, the old man had already
          disappeared.
I tell you this with a smile:
It's a very good poem.
It makes me jealous. You told me
my only weakness is loving you, and there's nothing I can do
about it.
By the way, my love, I have many things to do today.
By tomorrow I have to finish two pieces of writing!

Notes on the Poems

Page 20: According to the *Talmud*, an angel teaches babies all wisdom while they are in their mother's womb. Just before they are born, the angel touches them under their noses, and tells them to forget everything they were taught. The philtrum is formed by the angel's touch.

Page 36: On January 20, 2009, a fire broke out in the Nam Il Dang building in the Yongsan area of Seoul. The building was occupied by several protesters fighting against the forced eviction of poor occupants in the area, which was scheduled for construction of several luxury apartment complexes and other buildings. Five protesters and one riot police officer died in the fire, and twenty-four others were injured. The cause of the fire and the actions of the riot police are still under dispute: witnesses said the riot police used excessive force and ignored the screams of those trapped by the fire, but a court ruled that firebombs thrown on the roof of the building by protesters caused the disaster. Nine surviving protesters were given prison terms of up to six years.

Page 43: An Archimedean point (or "Punctum Archimedis") is a hypothetical vantage point from which an observer can objectively perceive the subject of inquiry, with a view of totality.

Page 46: Prometheus was the Titan god of forethought and crafty counsel who was entrusted with the task of moulding mankind out of clay. He dreamed of bettering the lives of his creation and tricked the gods out of the best portion of a sacrificial feast, acquiring the meat for the feasting of man. When Zeus withheld fire, he stole it from heaven and delivered it to mankind.

Page 52: According to BoSeon Shim, "Mundi" is his nickname for his lover. In this particular poem, he says, the subject of the poem can be his lover, or the world, or even his poetic muse.

Page 57: "Black Stone on a White Stone" is a poem by Peruvian poet Cesar Vallejo (1892-1938). In Santiago de Chuco, the homeland of Vallejo, they put a black stone on a white stone to signify a burial.

Page 83: Stephen Haggard (1911-1943) was a British poet, playwright and actor. He was once a very popular actor, but World War II interrupted his career. A few months after the North Africa campaign ended, and after a failed romance in Egypt, heartbroken and discouraged, he committed suicide on a train at the age of thirty-one.

About the Trsnslators

YoungShil Ji and Daniel T. Parker are a married translation team living in Daegu, South Korea. Ji graduated from Keimyung University and is a freelance translator specializing in contemporary Korean poetry. Parker was a journalist for thirteen years. He has an M.A. in English Literature from Murray State University in Kentucky and taught at Murray State, Paducah Community College, the University of Tennessee-Martin and Austin Peay State University in Clarksville, Tennessee, from 1993-2001. He has taught at Keimyung University since 2001 and is currently an assistant professor for the English Language & Literature department. *Wild Apple* (2015; White Pine Press) was their first poetry publication; they are currently working on a book by EunYoung Jin.

Korean Voices Series

Wild Apple
Poems by HeeDuk Ra
Translated by Daiel Parker and YoungShil Ji
Volume 21   978-1-934210-73-3   90 pages $17.99

Modern Family
A Novel by Cheon Myeong-Kwan
Translated by Kyoung-lee Park
Volume 20   978-1-934210-67-2   180 pages $16.00

I Must Be the Wind
Poems by Moon Chung-hee
Translated by Clare You and Richard Silberg
Volume 19   978-1-935210-60-3   118 pages $16.00

One Day, Then Another
Poems by Kim Kwang-Kyu
Translated by Cho Young-Shil
Volume 18   978-1-935210-54-2   104 pages $16.00

Magnolia & Lotus: Selected Poems of Hyesim
Translated by Ian Haight and T'ae-yong Ho
Volume 17   978-1-935210-43-6   96 pages $16.00

This Side of Time: Selected Poems by Ko Un
Translated by Claire You and Richard Silberg
Volume 16   978-1-935210-32-0   100 pages $16.00

Borderland Roads: Selected Poems of Ho Kyun
Translated by Ian Haight and T'ae-yong Ho
Volume 15   978-1-935210-08-5   102 pages $16.00

Brother Enemy: Poems of the Korean War
Edited and translated by Suh Ji-moon
Volume 6   1-893996-20-4   176 pages $16.00

Shrapnel and Other Stories
Stories of Dong-ha Lee
Translated by Hyun-jae Yee Sallee
Volume 5   1-893996-53-0   176 pages $16.00

Strong Wind At Mishi Pass
Poems by Tong-gyu Hwang
Translated by Seong-kon Kim & Dennis Maloney
Volume 4   1-893996-10-7   118 pages $15.00

A Sketch of the Fading Sun
Stories of Wan-suh Park
Translated by Hyun-jae Yee Sallee
Volume 3   1-877727-93-8   200 pages $15.00

Heart's Agony: Selected Poems of Chiha Kim
Translated by Won-chun Kim and James Han
Volume 2   1-877727-84-9   128 pages $14.00

The Snowy Road: An Anthology of Korean Fiction
Translated by Hyun-jae Yee Sallee
Volume 1   1-877727-19-9   168 pages $12.00